FROM SEA to SHINING SEA

NEVADA

SUZANNE M. WILLIAMS

Consultants

MELISSA N. MATUSEVICH, PH.D.

Curriculum and Instruction Specialist
Blacksburg, Virginia

ANNE B. AAS, M.L.I.S.

Librarian
Washoe County School District
Reno, Nevada

CORY KING

Youth Services Librarian
Carson City Library
Carson City, Nevada

CHILDREN'S PRESS®

A DIVISION OF SCHOLASTIC INC.

New York • Toronto • London • Auckland • Sydney • Mexico City
New Delhi • Hong Kong • Danbury, Connecticut

Nevada is in the southwestern part of the United States. It is bordered by California, Oregon, Idaho, Utah, and Arizona.

The photograph on the front cover shows a road through the Valley of Fire State Park.

Project Editor: Meredith DeSousa
Art Director: Marie O'Neill
Photo Researcher: Marybeth Kavanagh
Design: Robin West, Ox and Company, Inc.
Page 6 map and recipe art: Susan Hunt Yule
All other maps: XNR Productions, Inc.

Library of Congress Cataloging-in-Publication Data

Williams, Suzanne, 1949–
      Nevada / Suzanne Williams.
        p. cm. – (From sea to shining sea)
      Includes bibliographical references (p.) and index.
      Contents: Introducing the Silver State – The land of Nevada – Nevada through History
– Governing Nevada – The people and places of Nevada – Nevada almanac – Timeline –
Gallery of famous Nevadans.
   ISBN 0-516-22488-3
    1. Nevada—Juvenile literature. [1. Nevada.] I. Title. II. Series.

F841.3.W555 2003
979.3—dc21   2003000368

TABLE of CONTENTS

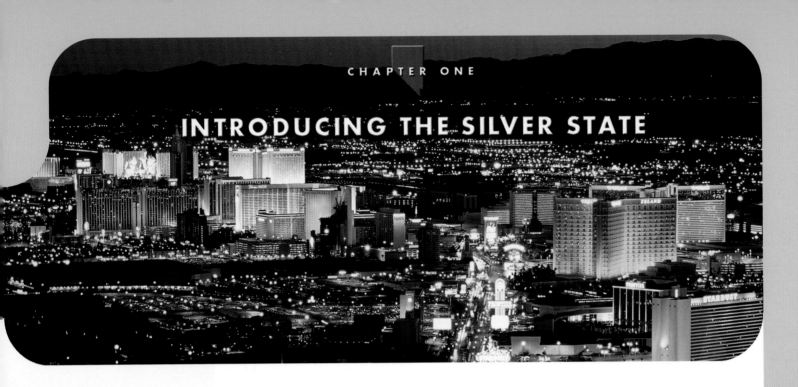

CHAPTER ONE

INTRODUCING THE SILVER STATE

Las Vegas is one of the fastest-growing cities in the United States.

Do you want to see wild horses, explore ghost towns, and search for unidentified flying objects (UFOs)? You can do all of these things in Nevada. You can also see Native American petroglyphs, or rock carvings, and watch Top Gun pilots practice flying fighter jets above Fallon Naval Air Station. You can listen to cowboy poetry in Elko, or drive for miles across the Extraterrestrial Highway. In September, watch hundreds of hot-air balloons lift off above Reno. Then cheer for camels and their riders at the wacky Virginia City Camel Races. All of these things and more can be found in Nevada.

The word *Nevada* means "snowy" in Spanish. You might think of Nevada as a hot desert state. Most of the state is dry, but it isn't always hot. In winter, most of the mountains in northern and central Nevada are topped with snow.

Nevada is nicknamed the Silver State. Miners came to Nevada in the 1850s looking for gold and silver. During the next twenty years, they took more than one billion dollars in silver and gold from the Comstock, near Virginia City. Nevada silver helped pay for the Civil War and helped to build the city of San Francisco, California. In fact, silver helped the Nevada Territory to become a state in 1864.

Today's Nevada is full of surprises. It has bristlecone pines, the oldest living things on earth. It also has ghost towns and the bustling city of Las Vegas. Near Las Vegas, you can tour Hoover Dam, one of the world's highest concrete dams. Then hike through the twisted red boulders at Valley of Fire State Park.

What else comes to mind when you think of Nevada?

- Mountain lakes
- Symphony orchestras
- Working cattle ranches
- Native American communities
- Dinosaur bones
- Modern mines
- Military bases

Nevada is a special combination of the Old West spirit and modern-day opportunities. This unique mix attracts all kinds of folks, including artists, gamblers, cowboys, and businesspeople, making Nevada one of the fastest-growing states. Welcome to the Silver State!

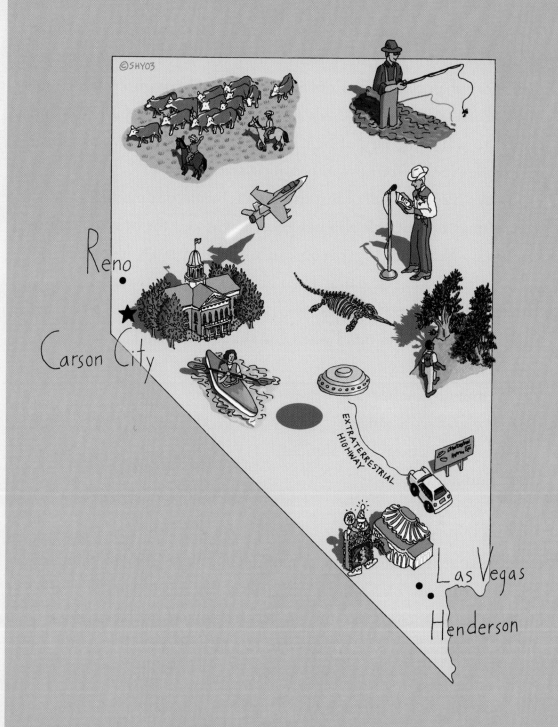

Reno

Carson City

EXTRATERRESTRIAL HIGHWAY

Las Vegas

Henderson

©SHY03

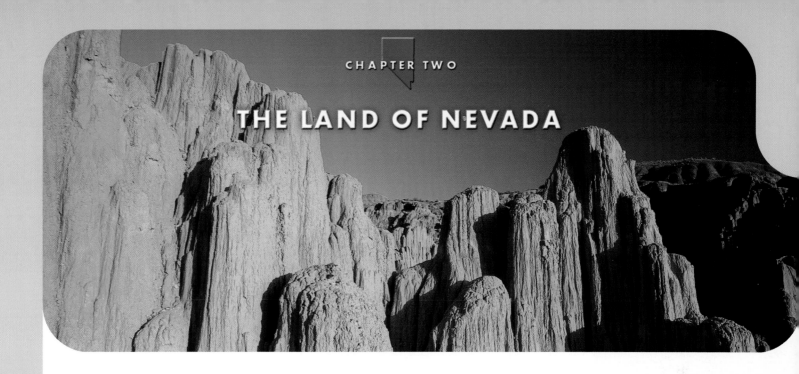

CHAPTER TWO

THE LAND OF NEVADA

Nevada is a wedge-shape state in the western part of the United States. It is bordered by California to the west and south, Oregon and Idaho to the north, and Utah and Arizona to the east. Nevada has 110,567 square miles (286,367 square kilometers) of land, making it the seventh largest state.

Nevada's landscape includes spectacular geologic formations such as Cathedral Gorge.

BASIN AND RANGE

Nevada has hundreds of mountain ranges. Most run from north to south. The valleys in between are called basins. Much of Nevada land is called the Basin and Range.

The Basin and Range landscape began forming about twenty million years ago

EXTRA! EXTRA!

Millions of years ago, much of Nevada was underwater. Giant ichthyosaurs, dinosaurs that look like fish, swam in seas that covered what is now central Nevada. Today, you can visit Berlin Ichthyosaur State Park and see skeletons of some of the largest ichthyosaurs that have been found. Some grew as long as 50 feet (15 meters). Now their fossils lie on a mountain among juniper and pine trees.

Hot water erupts from a geyser in the Black Rock Desert.

Sagebrush covers more than half of Nevada's land.

when the earth's crust started to stretch. The top layers tore, leaving mountains (ranges) with low spots (basins) in between. The earth's crust has been stretched thin across many basins. Hot rocks and gases below the earth's surface heat water that is trapped underground. In some places, the water bubbles to the surface in hot springs.

There is more than hot water underground. There are also many mines in Nevada's mountains. Nevada produces more precious metals than any other state. In 1997, Nevada produced $2.72 billion worth of gold and silver. Other materials, such as copper, barite, cement, gypsum, and limestone, are also mined in the state.

Within the Basin and Range region lies a desert area called the Great Basin. Most areas are covered with sweet-smelling sagebrush, which dots the land like a gray-green blanket. High altitudes create islands of life. There is snow on the mountains. Creeks tumble down canyons. Piñon pine and juniper trees grow on mountainsides. Cottonwoods, willows, and aspens line riverbeds.

Water attracts birds and other wildlife. Great flocks gather in spring and fall as they fly north and south. American white pelicans nest near Great Basin lakes. Scarlet ibis—huge stilt-legged, red-backed birds—can fill a marsh. Yellow-headed blackbirds live along irrigation ditches. Deer, antelope, coyotes, beavers, muskrats, rabbits, and raccoons make their homes near the water, too.

Some land is bare. Rocks and gravel spill down slopes. There are rocky cliffs, sand dunes, and *playas,* which are old lake bottoms. When the water evaporated, salt was left behind, preventing almost anything from growing there. Playas are flat, hard, and smooth. The Black Rock Desert, north of Reno, is part of the bottom of Lake Lahontan. The Bonneville Salt Flats begin at Nevada's eastern border near Wendover and cross into Utah on the dry lake bed of ancient Lake Bonneville.

The Black Rock Desert is a playa surrounded by mountains. The flat playa bed dries out in summer.

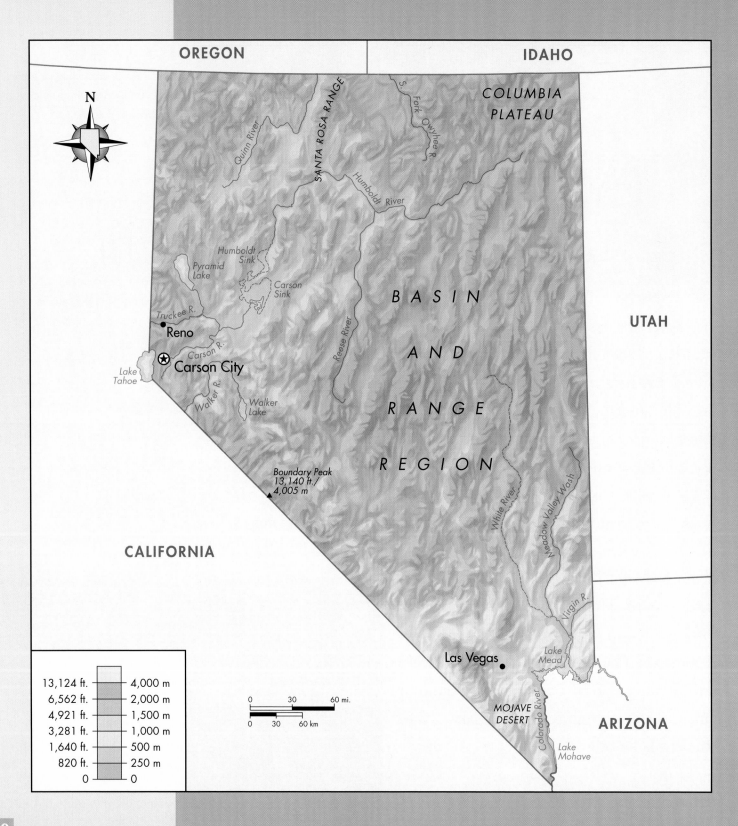

OREGON

IDAHO

N

COLUMBIA PLATEAU

Quinn River

SANTA ROSA RANGE

S. Fork Owyhee R.

Humboldt River

Humboldt Sink

Pyramid Lake

Carson Sink

Reese River

Truckee R.

● Reno

Carson R.

✪ Carson City

Lake Tahoe

UTAH

B A S I N

A N D

R A N G E

R E G I O N

Walker R.

Walker Lake

Boundary Peak
13,140 ft./
4,005 m
▲

White River

Meadow Valley Wash

CALIFORNIA

Virgin R.

Las Vegas ●

Lake Mead

Colorado River

MOJAVE DESERT

ARIZONA

Lake Mohave

13,124 ft.		4,000 m
6,562 ft.		2,000 m
4,921 ft.		1,500 m
3,281 ft.		1,000 m
1,640 ft.		500 m
820 ft.		250 m
0		0

0   30   60 mi.

0   30   60 km

COLUMBIA PLATEAU

A small corner of northeast Nevada is part of the Columbia Plateau. Water from this area goes to the Columbia River. Sagebrush and pine trees grow there, mountains tower above quiet lakes, and dirt roads lead to rocky canyons, as they do in the Great Basin.

MOJAVE DESERT

Southern Nevada is in the Mojave Desert. The Mojave Desert covers parts of Nevada, California, Arizona, and Utah. In Nevada, it is hard to tell exactly where the Great Basin ends and the Mojave begins. One way is to look at the plants. Different plants grow in the warmer Mojave Desert, including yucca and cholla cactus. Creosote bush replaces sagebrush as you travel south. Forests of Joshua trees grow on hillsides. (Religious Mormon explorers named them Joshua trees

Several species of yucca grow in the Mojave Desert, including the Mojave yucca, shown here.

because they thought their upright "arms" looked like the biblical figure Joshua praying.)

In southern Nevada, layers of red and white rocks were created 150 million years ago. Rain, wind, and the waters of the Colorado River have since uncovered them. At Valley of Fire State Park, east of Las Vegas, red rocks twist into amazing shapes, such as beehives and elephant rocks.

THE SIERRA NEVADA AND RIVER VALLEYS

The western edge of Nevada is close to the Sierra Nevada Mountains. This range is steep and rocky. Nevada's highest point is Boundary Peak, in the White Mountains, near the Sierra Nevada. It stands 13,140 feet (4,005

Winter snow collects on Boundary Peak in the White Mountains.

meters). The mountains are covered with pine, fir, cedar, and aspen trees. From fall through early summer, the granite peaks of the Sierra Nevada are covered with snow. Rivers that start in the mountains bring water to valleys in western Nevada. Meadows and marshes make homes for birds, coyotes, rabbits, antelope, and deer.

THE EASTERN BORDER—HIGHLANDS, CANYONS, AND WASHES

The eastern border of Nevada is mountainous, too. Eastern Nevada mountains usually get more rain and snow than mountains in the center of the state. The Ruby Mountains, near Elko, get an average of about 32 inches (81 centimeters) of precipitation each year. Mountains along the eastern border are covered with piñon pines and juniper trees. Travel up the mountains and you'll come across aspen groves and beaver dams.

Bristlecone pines, the world's oldest living plants, grow on Wheeler Peak in Great Basin National Park, near Ely. The sun lights up the chalky spires of Cathedral Gorge. Peach, lilac, and white rocks line the sides of Rainbow Canyon. Most days, a small creek trickles along its bottom, but don't be fooled. Rainbow Canyon is a wash—a desert riverbed that is usually dry. When summer thunderstorms pound the mountains above a wash, the water pours in, creating a flash flood. Rainbow Canyon has had many flash floods.

The unusual form of a bristlecone pine adds to the wild and beautiful scenery of Great Basin National Park.

Most of Nevada lies within the Great Basin, a huge low spot surrounded by mountains, like a basin or sink. Rain that falls in the Great Basin stays there. Rivers run down its mountains toward the bottom of the basin. The rivers end in lakes or in sinks, which are swampy areas. Because water flows into the lakes but does not flow out, they are called terminal lakes. Some terminal lakes become salty as water evaporates, leaving salts behind.

Lake Lahontan was a terminal lake that once covered about 8,000 square miles (20,720 sq km). Birds and animals lived along its shores. Large trees grew on nearby mountains. Waves along its shores carved terraces, or flat places, and caves. Then the climate began to get hotter and drier, and Lake Lahontan began to dry up.

The Walker River provides water for many farmers and ranchers in western Nevada.

Today, all that remains of ancient Lake Lahontan are smaller lakes such as Pyramid and Walker lakes in western Nevada. The Walker River tumbles 160 miles (257 km) down the eastern Sierra Nevada into Walker Lake. The Carson River and the Humboldt River disappear into the desert in sinks. Water in a sink evaporates, or dries up, fast enough that a real lake never forms. The river simply stops.

The Truckee River begins at Lake Tahoe. Water from Lake Tahoe runs down the Truckee River into Pyramid Lake. The water stays in Pyramid Lake until it evaporates.

Some Nevada rivers don't flow into the Great Basin. The 1,450-mile-(2,334-km-) long Colorado River runs from Colorado to Mexico. Part of it forms the border between Nevada and Arizona. Hoover Dam traps Colorado River water to form Lake Mead, a huge man-made lake on the Nevada-Arizona border. The Owyhee River runs from the northeast corner of Nevada into the Snake River. Water in the Snake flows to the Columbia River and then to the Pacific Ocean.

Some lakes and rivers in Nevada do a disappearing act. During the winter, rains fill shallow lakes in the basin areas. During the dry summer, they disappear. Some lake beds are dry for years and reappear after a wet winter. Many Nevada riverbeds fill only after rainstorms.

EXTRA! EXTRA!

Lake Tahoe lies half in California and half in Nevada. It is 12 miles (19 km) wide and 22 miles (35 km) long, and it averages 1,000 feet (305 m) deep, making it the largest alpine lake in North America. There is enough water in Lake Tahoe to cover all of Nevada with 20 inches (51 cm) of water.

CLIMATE

Nevada is the driest state. Nevada's average rainfall is 9 inches (23 cm), but much of the state receives less than 8 inches (20 cm) per year. Many

The mountains block moisture in many parts of Nevada, creating a desert climate.

Sierra peaks are more than 10,000 feet (3,048 m) high and create a rain shadow, an area where little rain or snow falls.

Most rainstorms come from the west. Storms rain heavily on the west side of the Sierra Nevada mountains. The clouds warm as they come down the east side of the mountains into Nevada. Warm air holds more water than cold air, and so the rain stops. Mount Rose, west of Reno, gets an average of 51 inches (130 cm) of precipitation per year. (Precipitation is rain and snow measured as water.) Reno, in the rain shadow, receives just 7.5 inches (19 cm). Most precipitation falls as winter snow. In some parts of northern and eastern Nevada, snow can stay on the ground for most of the winter.

Most of Nevada is more than 4,000 feet (1,219 m) above sea level. Nevada's high altitude and clear skies create large temperature ranges. The land heats up during sunny days, but without clouds to trap the heat, the air cools quickly at night. The average summer daytime temperature in Reno is 91° Fahrenheit (33° Celsius). In January, it is 45° F (7° C). Southern Nevada is usually warmer than the northern part of the state. Average high temperatures in Las Vegas are 105° F (41° C) in July and 56° F (13° C) in January.

CHAPTER THREE

NEVADA THROUGH HISTORY

The first people in Nevada may have arrived more than 12,000 years ago. Their ancestors probably made a long journey from Asia to North America. These people, called Paleo-Indians, traveled to different parts of North and South America, including Nevada.

Scientists have discovered signs of these early people, such as bone tools found at Tule Springs, near Las Vegas, that may be 13,000 years old. Some early Indians also drew petroglyphs, or drawings carved into rock. These drawings are found in many places in Nevada. They show animals, people, and other things, but no one knows exactly what these drawings mean. Early people probably hunted birds and animals around Nevada's lakes and marshes. They gathered plants to eat.

This illustration shows a view of the Nevada state capitol in 1878.

These petroglyphs in Valley of Fire State Park provide clues about the lives of ancient people.

The Lovelock Cave People (1000 B.C.) lived near Lake Lahontan in western Nevada. Scientists found many of their belongings in a cave near present-day Lovelock. From studying these objects, they learned that Lovelock people hunted small animals with darts, wove nets for catching rabbits, and made tule duck decoys. They made the decoys by weaving tules, or reeds, into duck shapes, then floated them on the lake to attract real ducks. Today's Northern Paiute people make tule duck decoys, too.

The Basket Makers (50 B.C.–A.D. 500) lived in southern Nevada, near the Virgin and Muddy rivers. They wove baskets and sandals out of plants. They lived in circular pit houses dug below the ground. The roofs of the houses were just above the ground and were covered with brush or reeds.

The Basket Makers were probably ancestors of the Anasazi, a group of people who lived in the area from about A.D. 500–1150. The Anasazi lived in many parts of the Southwest, including present-day Colorado, Utah, Arizona, New Mexico, and the southern tip of Nevada. They built a village called Lost City on the Muddy River near Overton. Their houses, called pueblos, had many rooms, sometimes as many as one

EXTRA! EXTRA!

When Hoover Dam was built in the 1930s, the remains of a nearby Anasazi village were in danger of being lost. To protect the village's valuable artifacts from the waters of Lake Mead, the U.S. National Park Service moved as many tools, baskets, and pots as possible. When Hoover Dam was finished, water rose over the village, and it disappeared underwater. Some of the things that were saved are on display at the Lost City Museum (above) in Overton.

hundred. In Nevada, they used rocks and adobe—bricks made from mud and straw—to build pueblos.

The Anasazi hunted animals and irrigated crops of corn, squash, and beans. They built an underground salt mine at Lost City. The Anasazi at Lost City may have traded salt for other things, such as pottery, with other Anasazi groups. The Anasazi villages disappeared around 1150.

By the early 1800s, five Native American groups lived in Nevada. They were the Southern Paiute, the Northern Paiute, the Mojave, the Western Shoshone, and the Washo. Southern Paiutes and Mojaves lived in the southern tip of Nevada. They hunted small animals and gathered seeds and plants to eat. They also grew crops such as squash, beans, and melons along the rivers.

The Western Shoshone and the Northern Paiute lived in the Great Basin. They moved around gathering food. Northern Paiutes built shelters and houses out of reeds and grasses. When a band moved, they left the shelters behind. Houses woven from willows or cattails might last a few years. The Paiutes wove nets to catch rabbits and made duck decoys and rafts from the reeds that grew in lakes and marshes. Women wove baskets

This illustration by Karen Beyers shows Paiutes gathering pine nuts and grasses.

from willows and grasses. Men made traps from rocks balanced on trigger sticks to catch birds, rabbits, and other small animals. In the fall, everyone gathered pine nuts from piñon pine trees.

The Washo people lived near Lake Tahoe in Nevada and California. Like the Northern Paiute and Shoshone people, they made baskets, hunted small animals, and gathered pine nuts. However, they spoke a language different from the Northern Paiute and Shoshone. All of these Native American groups knew how to live in the desert.

SPANISH AND MEXICAN EXPLORERS

Europeans began exploring North America in the 1500s. The Spanish settled Santa Fe, New Mexico, in 1610. In the 1700s, priests built missions, or religious settlements, along California's coast. In 1775 and 1776, Spanish explorers Francisco Garcés and Fathers Francisco Dominguez and Silvestre Escalante explored just east and south of Nevada, in today's Arizona and California.

In 1821, Mexico won its freedom from Spain. Today's Southwest, including Nevada, became part of Mexico. However, few Mexicans lived in the northern part of Mexico. The largest northern settlements were in Santa Fe and California.

In 1829, José Antonio Armijo led a group from Santa Fe to southern California. Armijo's group rested by a grassy spring along the way. They named the spot Las Vegas, Spanish for "the meadows." Armijo's route was called the Old Spanish Trail. People used it to travel between the town of Santa Fe and the missions in southern California. Las Vegas became a camping stop on the Old Spanish Trail.

AMERICAN AND BRITISH EXPLORERS

While Mexico owned today's Southwest, Mexicans still lived mostly in California and today's New Mexico. A small number of Mexicans had to protect Mexico's claim to a huge area. At this time, the United States went from the Atlantic coast to the Missouri River, and it wasn't long before U.S. explorers began to enter the Southwest.

Most early explorers were fur trappers who came in search of beavers and otters. Trappers could make lots of money selling beaver and otter furs in eastern cities and in Europe. Jedediah Smith was a trapper and explorer who worked for the Rocky Mountain Fur Company. He led the first group of United States trappers to cross Nevada in 1826 and 1827. Another trapper, Peter Skene Ogden, worked for the British-owned Hudson's Bay Company. He and his men were based near the Columbia River in today's Oregon. Between 1825 and 1835, Ogden's group traveled south into Nevada, hunting animals for furs.

In the 1830s, there were twenty-four states. All the states, except Missouri, were

Fur trader Jedediah Smith was a trailblazer through the American West.

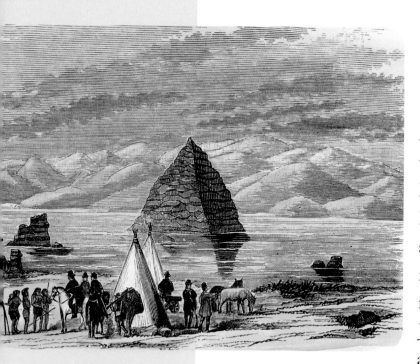

John Frémont and his men set up camp at Pyramid Lake during their journey west.

east of the Mississippi River. However, United States politicians believed that the country was meant to own land from the Atlantic to the Pacific oceans. This belief was referred to as Manifest Destiny. To learn more about the land west of the Rockies, the United States government sent John Frémont, a soldier and map-maker, to explore the area. Frémont hired famous mountain men Kit Carson and Joseph Walker to guide him. He crossed and mapped Nevada in 1843 and 1845. Frémont named two Nevada rivers, the Carson and the Walker, for his guides. His detailed maps and journals helped people to learn about the West.

THE EMIGRANT TRAIL

As people learned more about the West, many wanted to move there. Pioneers packed their wagons and headed west in wagon trains. Some went in search of good farmland and others went to find gold, which was discovered in California in 1848. Between 1840 and 1860, thousands of people traveled the Emigrant Trail across Nevada to California.

In Nevada, pioneers followed the Humboldt River until the water disappeared in the Humboldt Sink. Next, they crossed the Forty-Mile

Desert. This flat, dry 40-mile (64-km) stretch of land lay between the end of the Humboldt River and the next water source. Horses and oxen died. Emigrants tossed aside their belongings to lighten their loads. Dead animals, bones, and other objects lined the trail. In 1852, pioneer John Hawkins Clark wrote, "About ten miles out the dead teams of 1849 and 1850 were seen scattered here and there on the road . . . in a little while they filled the entire roadside . . . Wagons, wagon irons, ox chains, harness, rifles, . . . lay scattered along this notorious route, reminding one of the defeat of some great army."

EXTRA! EXTRA!

Not every pioneer completed the journey. In 1846, a group of eighty-seven people led by George Donner left the Midwest on their way to California. The Donner Party took a new northern route across Nevada, hoping it would be a shortcut. That winter, a huge snowstorm trapped the group near Donner Lake, just across the Nevada border in California.

Fifteen people went for help. Seven lived, arriving at Sutter's Fort near today's Sacramento, California. By the time rescuers could get back to the others, in late February 1847, many people had died. The survivors had eaten dead livestock, shoes, and even the bodies of people who had died. Forty-six members of the Donner Party lived. Donner Pass and Donner Lake, in California, are named for them.

A NEW WAY OF LIFE

The emigrants didn't cross an empty land. Western Shoshone and Northern Paiute people lived in the Great Basin. Horses and cattle from the wagon trains ate the sparse desert plants, and pioneers killed game to eat, making it difficult for Indians to find food. Emigrants camped by the rivers. Dead animals and waste fouled the water. Typhoid, a disease carried in dirty water, killed pioneers and Paiutes.

Although most Paiutes tried to stay out of the newcomers' way, Paiute Chief Truckee thought his people would have to learn about the new settlers in order to get along with them. Chief Truckee made friends with mapmaker and soldier John Frémont.

As more and more settlers moved west, the United States government wanted ownership of the area. California, Nevada, Utah, Colorado, Arizona, New Mexico, and parts of Wyoming belonged to Mexico. In the spring of 1846, fighting broke out on the Texas-Mexico border. In June, United States settlers in California revolted against the Mexican government. The Mexican-American War (1846–1848) had begun. John Frémont led troops in California, and Chief Truckee joined 400 Native Americans from the Great Basin and California who fought with Frémont. Two years later, the United States won the war and took control of today's Southwest.

PASSING THROUGH

In 1848, gold was discovered at Sutter's Mill near Sacramento, California. When word got out, it wasn't long before the Emigrant Trail became flooded with miners who wanted California gold. Between 1840 and 1860, more than 200,000 people traveled the Emigrant Trail on their way to California.

Gold also helped some mountain men to make a fortune. James Beckwourth was a famous trail guide and trapper. In 1850, he found a path from the Truckee Meadows (present-day Reno) across a low pass into California. Beckwourth Pass was one of the best ways to cross the Sierra Nevada. Many travelers bought supplies from Beckwourth.

Not every traveler went to California, however. Mormons—members of the Church of Jesus Christ of Latter-day Saints—were Nevada's first non-Native American settlers. In 1850, the Mormons built Mormon Station at present-day Genoa.

A few years earlier, Mormon leader Brigham Young led thousands of Latter-day Saints to Utah. Mormons had been driven out of many states because of their religious beliefs. Once safely in Utah, Young imagined creating a new country for Latter-day Saints called Deseret. He hoped it would stretch from Salt Lake to southern California. The church sent groups, including the settlers at Mormon Station, south and west to settle the area.

The Mormons trekked across wind-blown plains and frozen mountain valleys to find a place where they could freely practice their religion.

In 1855, the church sent thirty men to Las Vegas springs. They farmed and preached to the Native Americans. One man wrote that the dry, rocky country "looks as though the Lord has forgotten it." Mission life was hard. The men were far from other settlements, and sometimes their crops failed and they went hungry. In 1858, the Las Vegas mission closed.

Before long, non-Mormon settlers in Utah began to complain about Mormon leadership and government. The United States government also spoke out. Some leaders thought Mormons were living by their their own rules and not those of the United States. In 1857, President James Buchanan sent 2,500 soldiers to take over Salt Lake City. Brigham Young called all Mormons, including those in Nevada, back to Salt Lake City to fight. The government and the Mormons were able to agree on new rules without fighting. However, Mormon settlers left western Utah Territory (Nevada) just before thousands of non-Mormons poured in.

THE COMSTOCK STRIKE

As the California Gold Rush ended, miners looked for gold in nearby places. They found gold in an area of Nevada known as Washoe. In 1859, silver was discovered there, too. Miners rushed to the area. They built Virginia City, on Mount Davidson, near the mines. Eight hundred buildings went up the first year, including houses, stores, schools, and churches. Timber from nearby Franktown and Lake Tahoe supported the mine shafts and built the town.

Miners took almost one billion dollars of gold and silver from the mines during the next twenty years. Nevada's rich strike was named the Comstock Lode for Henry Paige Comstock, who claimed to own the land where some of the first silver was found. Comstock silver was deep inside Mount Davidson. Some mines were 1,300 feet (396 m) below ground, and engineers had to invent ways to get the metal. Philip Deidesheimer created square-rigged timbers, or timbers built into huge boxlike shapes, to hold the mines. Adolf Sutro built a tunnel at the base of Mount Davidson to drain water from the mines.

Mining companies made huge profits. They hired miners to dig tunnels, smash hard rock, and place huge timbers deep underground. The mines were dark, flooded with water, and hot from geothermal activity. Most miners didn't get rich, although Virginia City miners were paid better than miners in other places.

Miners worked hundreds of feet below ground under dangerous conditions to access the precious metals.

THE PAIUTE WAR

In 1860, about 6,800 nonnative people lived in Nevada. By the 1870s, Virginia City alone had a population of about 20,000. People from around the world came to western Nevada to work in the mines.

WHO'S WHO IN NEVADA?

Sarah Winnemucca (1844–1891) was the daughter of Paiute Chief Winnemucca. Her family sent her to live with the family of Carson City leader Major William Ormsby so that she could learn the newcomers' ways. As an adult, she translated Native American languages for the U.S. Army and began a school for Paiute children in Lovelock. In 1883, she wrote *Life Among the Paiutes,* the first book by a Native American woman. Winnemucca was born near Humboldt Sink in western Nevada.

Paiutes (right) and the settlers clashed as more Americans moved in and took over the land.

The fragile desert could not support everyone, however. Miners cut down trees, including piñon pines that Paiute, Shoshone, and Washo people used for nuts. More people were hunting animals for food. Miners and settlers built their houses near water where Native Americans hunted.

The western Nevada Indians and the newcomers did not trust each other. In May 1860, Native Americans killed two or three settlers living near the Carson River. They said that these men had kidnapped two young Paiute girls.

Miners and settlers were scared. They gathered about one hundred men and rode toward Pyramid Lake to punish the Paiutes. The Paiutes attacked first, killing seventy-six settlers. Soldiers and volunteers came from California to fight. About 700 men attacked the Pyramid Lake Paiutes again.

The Paiute War lasted three months. The Paiutes lost. As part of the peace treaty, the Paiutes agreed to give up most of their land to the settlers, but they kept the Pyramid Lake Reservation for themselves. By 1867, however, settlers had taken much of the best farmland on the reservation.

As the United States continued to grow, it became more of a challenge for people in different parts of the country to communicate with one another. In April 1860, the Pony Express began. The Pony Express used a relay of horse riders to deliver mail from one place to another. It promised what was considered fast delivery—letters would arrive in California in ten days instead of the usual thirty. Pony Express riders carried mail from St. Joseph, Missouri, to Sacramento, California, racing about 33 miles (53 km) between stations.

While riders galloped with the mail, other people were building a telegraph line. The telegraph would carry messages over a wire as a series of electrical clicks. The line was finished on October 24, 1861—a year and a half after the Pony Express began. These instant telegraph messages replaced the Pony Express.

Soon, messages were filled with news of another war. In the eastern United States, the North and the South were arguing about slavery. In the South, many people treated African-Americans and other slaves as property. They forced them to do the hardest work. Many northern states were against the spread of slavery and had outlawed it. These were known as free states. Both free states and slave states (those that allowed slavery) wanted new western states on their side.

Abraham Lincoln, elected president in 1860, was against any new territory allowing slavery. In December 1860, South Carolina seceded from, or left, the Union. Other southern states followed. Together they created a new nation called the Confederate States of America.

James Nye governed the Nevada Territory until 1864. Nye County is named for him.

For many years, slave-state representatives had stopped free territories and states in the West from joining the Union. However, by 1861, many southern slave states had left the Union. In 1861, outgoing president James Buchanan created the free Nevada Territory. A few weeks later, the new president, Abraham Lincoln, appointed Nevada's first territorial governor, James Nye.

In 1861, the Civil War (1861–1865) began. President Lincoln knew that Nevada's silver could pay for guns and food to support the war. If Nevada became a state, its silver would belong to the Union. Also, Lincoln believed that congressmen from the new state would support a change to the constitution outlawing slavery. Timing was important. The decision would be made soon. In September 1864, Nevadans approved the state constitution. State leaders telegraphed the constitution to Washington, D.C., and Lincoln declared Nevada the thirty-sixth state on October 31, 1864. Carson City became the capital.

WHAT'S IN A NAME?

The names of many places in Nevada have interesting origins.

Name	Comes From or Means
Las Vegas	Spanish for "the meadows"
Reno	Named for Civil War officer Jesse Lee Reno
Tonopah	Paiute word for "small spring" or "greasewood by the water"
Virginia City	Named for miner "Old Virginia" Fennimore
Winnemucca	Named for Paiute chief Winnemucca

THE RAILROAD

Most people came to Nevada to mine. Boomtowns such as Aurora, Unionville, and Austin sprang up when prospectors found gold or silver. Aurora, near the California border, had 6,000 people and produced $30 million of ore (rocks containing precious metals).

People rushed to Nevada's mines from around the world. Italians, Greeks, Serbs, Irish, Chinese, and Basque people (from the Pyrenees Mountains between France and Spain) came to Nevada. When Basques first arrived in Nevada, they often found a home at a Basque hotel near the railroad station. There, they could speak their own language, eat Basque meals, and look for work. By the 1870s, nearly half of the 42,500 nonnative people in Nevada had been born in foreign countries.

Despite all this activity, California and Nevada were far away from the other states. A railroad across the continent would tie these rich western states to the rest of the Union. In the middle of the Civil War, the United States government decided to build a railroad that would span the continent. The tracks would cross central Nevada. In October 1863, the Central Pacific Railroad laid tracks east from Sacramento, and Union Pacific built west from Omaha, Nebraska.

In California and Nevada, Chinese laborers did the most dangerous jobs. Chinese men had come to the West to work in the mines. Now many of them worked on the railroad. They blasted out tunnels and hung in baskets over steep mountain cliffs to set dynamite charges. They often worked long hours for little pay.

Trains needed places to take on water, fuel, and freight. New towns, such as Reno and Battle Mountain, were built to service

The railroad provided a link to the rest of the country, making it easier for people to travel to Nevada.

the trains, load freight, and take care of passengers. Other towns, such as Winnemucca, already existed. When the railroad came through, new people moved in.

Despite the coming of the railroad, the state depended on silver. Although it was profitable for many years, Comstock silver didn't last forever. By 1878, it was almost gone. Other mining areas, such as Eureka in central Nevada, were producing less, too.

Some Nevadans raised cattle and sheep, but there wasn't enough water in most of Nevada for everyone to turn to farming. Stores closed. Lawyers didn't have clients. Teachers had fewer students. By 1890, one in three Nevadans had left the state. The population dropped from about 62,000 in 1880 to less than 48,000 in 1890. There was even talk of closing the state.

THE BANNOCK WAR

By the 1870s, few Native Americans in Nevada could manage to live by hunting and gathering. They were supposed to live on reservations, or land set aside for them by agreements made between the tribes and the United States government. Land on the reservations was often poor.

There wasn't enough land to hunt animals. The settlers' cattle ate roots and seeds they used for food. To escape, some Native Americans hid in the mountains and continued to hunt and gather there. Meanwhile, bands on the reservations went hungry.

In 1878, the United States government ordered Idaho's Bannock people to stay on their reservation. They refused. United States General George Crook said, "[It is] a question of war path or starvation, and . . . many of them will always choose [war] . . . when death shall at least be glorious." The Bannocks went to war so that they could hunt and gather as they always had. Some Paiutes from northern Nevada and Shoshones and Umitillas from eastern Oregon and Washington joined them. Other Paiutes fought alongside the United States Army.

The Bannock War lasted from May to August. The Bannocks lost. After the war, Paiutes from northern Nevada were ordered to leave the state. They were forced to walk 350 miles (563 km) to the Yakima Reservation in Washington State. Several women and children died on the trip. Years later, the Paiute were allowed to return to Fort McDermitt, near their original home.

Today, Northern Paiute reservations are at Pyramid Lake northeast of Reno, Walker River near Walker Lake, and Summit Lake in Humboldt County. The Paiute and Shoshone have reservations at Fort McDermitt in Humboldt County and Duck Valley in Elko County. Shoshones have reservations at Goshute in eastern Nevada, Duck Water southwest of Ely, and South Fork near Elko. The Washo have land at Dresslerville near Carson City. Southern Paiutes have a reservation at Moapa River near the Colorado River. Many of Nevada's Native Americans also live in cities and towns. Indian colonies, in many Nevada towns, are on Indian-controlled land.

WHO'S WHO IN NEVADA?

Wovoka (c. 1856–1932) was a Paiute spiritual leader. He believed that white people would disappear from North America and that Native Americans would live in peace. He encouraged his people not to hurt anyone and to dance the Ghost Dance to prepare for the coming salvation. Wovoka's Ghost Dance teachings spread across the Plains. Wovoka was born in Esmeralda County.

The main street of Tonopah was once filled with horse-drawn wagons bringing goods from one place to another.

In the 1900s, new strikes of silver at Tonopah, gold at Goldfield, and copper in White Pine County helped to revive Nevada. Goldfield produced at least $30 million worth of gold between 1904 and 1910.

In 1907, many residents of Goldfield worked for George Wingfield and George Nixon's Goldfield Consolidated Mining Company. Wingfield and Nixon suspected that miners were stealing gold ore. To prevent stealing, they made miners change their clothes before leaving the mines to be sure they weren't hiding anything. They also tried to pay miners with IOUs—papers that promised money later—instead of coins. Miners were angry.

Many miners joined together and formed a union, a group that works together to get better pay and treatment from company owners. At Goldfield, union members went on strike, or refused to work, until their demands were met. When production halted, United States Army troops were called in to keep order. Union members refused to go back to work, but most jobs were filled by non-union members. The union eventually lost power in Goldfield.

When the ore ran out in mining towns such as Goldfield, people packed up and left. When the ore ran out in Rhyolite, people even took their houses. There were few trees there, and wood was precious. People hauled the lumber from their houses and sold it to builders in the new town of Las Vegas.

To allow more people to live in the state, Nevada needed farms. Congressman Francis Newlands knew that water would turn Nevada deserts into farms, and in 1902, he convinced the United States government to create the Newlands Project. Workers built canals and dams on the Truckee and Carson rivers to bring water to new farms near today's Fernley and Fallon. Farmers could buy up to 160 acres (65 hectares) of land.

Dams built as part of the Newlands Project were used to irrigate western Nevada.

Although the project worked, it didn't provide enough water, and some farmers gave up. Also, as farmers used more water, less flowed to Pyramid Lake and Stillwater Marsh, causing fish and other wildlife to suffer. Today, Fernley and Fallon are farming communities. They still get their water from the Carson and Truckee river canals, but Nevadans continue to disagree over the uses of this water.

WORLD WAR I AND THE GREAT DEPRESSION

In 1917, the United States entered World War I (1914–1918). Nevada made many contributions to the war effort. More than 5,000 Nevadans fought in the war. Nevada's mines sold copper, silver, and lead for building weapons. Eastern Nevada's copper-mining companies sold $7 million worth of copper in 1914 and $25 million in 1916. Ranchers raised more cattle and sheep because they could get high prices for them.

Prosperity came to an end in 1929. That year the stock market crashed. People who had invested money in companies by buying stocks, or shares of a company, now found that their stocks were worthless. People all across the country lost money, and they could no longer afford to buy things. As a result, businesses lost money and often had to fire workers. So many people took their savings out of banks that the banks ran out of cash, and many closed. The Great Depression was a time of poverty that affected the entire United States, including Nevada.

Nevada's lawmakers tried to create jobs for people. In 1931, Nevada passed a law that made gambling—playing games for money—legal. Gambling became a major industry in the state, bringing jobs in hotels and casinos, places where people gamble.

Nevada also created new laws to attract visitors. At the time, it was difficult to get a divorce in most states. In 1931, state lawmakers changed the law to allow anyone who lived in the state for just six weeks to become a Nevadan, which meant they could get a divorce quickly. The new law attracted many people to Nevada, where they stayed for six weeks and got an easy divorce. In the meantime, they stayed in motels and ranches, and bought food, clothing, and other things in Nevada. The money they spent gave some Nevadans jobs.

The federal government created jobs in Nevada, too. In 1930, work began on Hoover Dam on the Colorado River. The dam would control floods, store water that farmers could use to irrigate fields, make electricity, and provide water to cities in the Southwest.

More than 5,000 workers from across the country came to build the dam. To accommodate the dam builders, the government built Boulder City, located 15 miles (24 km) from the dam. Boulder City had neat

Gambling houses were built throughout Nevada during the 1930s.

Constructed in 1931, Boulder City served as a "model" city for all of America.

rows of small houses, churches, a school, stores, a newspaper, and a police station. African-American workers were not allowed to live in Boulder City, however. They traveled more than 40 miles (64 km) to work every day from West Las Vegas. Chinese people were not hired at all.

Hoover Dam was finished in 1936. The water and electricity from the dam allowed Los Angeles, California; Phoenix, Arizona; and Las Vegas to grow.

WORLD WAR II

World War II (1939–1945) helped to end the Great Depression. The war broke out in Europe when Germany, which had been left broken and poor after World War I, attacked its neighbors. Japan sided with Germany. On December 7, 1941, Japan bombed a United States military base at Pearl Harbor in Hawaii. The United States entered the war the very next day. Men and women joined the military. Factories made weapons and war materials. Women, African-Americans, and Mexicans filled jobs left by the new soldiers.

About 21,000 Nevadans served in World War II. New military bases and factories drew people to Nevada. Nevada's mines produced metals that helped build planes, tanks, and other weapons. The United States government built a magnesium factory in Henderson, near Las Vegas. (Magnesium was used to build bombs.) Ten thousand people got jobs at the plant.

Thousands of airmen learned to fly at Nevada bases. Nellis Airbase opened north of Las Vegas. Reno Army Airbase (now Stead Air Force Base) and Fallon Naval Air Station also served as training centers.

THE MOB AND THE STRIP

In the 1940s, the Commercial Casino in Elko hired the first entertainment stars to perform in Nevada casinos. However, it was Las Vegas that became home to the stars. When money to build the Flamingo Hotel in Las Vegas ran out, a gangster named Benjamin "Bugsy" Siegel helped out. Many gangsters belonged to crime organizations in big cities such as New York, Chicago,

Gangster Bugsy Siegel helped build a lavish Las Vegas hotel called the Flamingo.

and Los Angeles. They made money from illegal drugs, gambling, and blackmail. Bugsy Siegel spent $6 million to finish the Flamingo.

Although crime organizations ran some Las Vegas casinos, many Hollywood stars came to Las Vegas to play and perform. Singer Frank Sinatra often sang at the Sands Hotel. He brought famous friends such as Sammy Davis Jr. and Dean Martin to perform, too. People began to think of Las Vegas as a "classy" place.

In 1967, billionaire Howard Hughes moved into the Desert Inn in Las Vegas. Hughes, a loner, rented the whole ninth floor of the hotel. Hughes later bought the hotel and several other Las Vegas casino/ hotels. Soon, other businesspeople bought casinos, and the state government began to enforce strict rules about gambling. Eventually, crime organizations lost their hold on Nevada casinos.

THE NEVADA TEST SITE

After World War II, the Las Vegas area continued to be important to the military. The United States and the Soviet Union became enemies. During the Cold War, both countries built powerful bombs to threaten one another. In 1951, the United States government began testing nuclear bombs at the Nevada Test Site, north of Las Vegas. This land was owned by the United States government.

Although the test site brought jobs to Nevada, people didn't know that radiation given off by the bombs was dangerous. Some people in Las Vegas had parties or sat outside to watch the excitement. People who lived

More than 900 nuclear weapons tests were performed at the Nevada Test Site between 1951 and 1992.

near the test site are called downwinders because the wind blew radiation from the bomb blasts to their communities. In 1963, the United States stopped exploding nuclear bombs above ground because of the effects of radiation. The tests continued underground until the 1990s.

EXTRA! EXTRA!

In the early 1900s, herds of wild horses, called mustangs, roamed Nevada. They sometimes ate grass that was needed for cattle, making them a problem for ranchers. Often, they were rounded up and sold for animal feed, or shot. Velma B. Johnston (nicknamed "Wild Horse Annie") led a national campaign to help protect the horses. In 1959, the Wild Horse Annie Bill was passed, outlawing the use of airplanes and other motorized vehicles to hunt down horses on federal lands; other laws followed. Today the Bureau of Land Management cares for extra horses and burros. The Wild Horse and Burro Adoption Center at Palomino Valley is one of two places wild horses are cared for; the other is in Nebraska. About half of the nation's 44,000 wild horses and burros live in Nevada.

Today, the United States government owns almost 9 in every 10 acres (3.6 in 4 ha) in Nevada. That means the government makes many decisions about Nevada's land and water. For example, the government can decide where cattle can graze and how much to charge ranchers for grazing. Many people feel that the officials making these decisions know little about Nevada.

In the 1980s, local governments began trying to gain control of these lands in what became known as the sagebrush rebellion. They demanded that the government sell federal land to Nevada so that local people could control it. Although that hasn't happened, many Nevadans still feel the national government has too much control of Nevada's lands.

The Western Shoshone Nation says that control is illegal. They say the Treaty of Ruby Valley, which its nation signed in 1863, never gave the United States legal rights to their land. The treaty allowed towns, ranches, mines, and roadways to be built, but the Shoshone say that their tribes did not give up control of the land. The Shoshone people have been arguing this case in court since 1935.

The United States government has another plan for Nevada land. It has decided to build a nuclear waste dump at Yucca Mountain. Radioactive nuclear waste from all over the country will be stored there. (Nuclear power plants, weapons factories, and medicine produce waste material that is radioactive.) The radiation lasts for 10,000 years.

The site is 100 miles (161 km) from Las Vegas. Many people think putting nuclear waste near a city is dangerous. Others hope the government will spend its money trying to find a way to make nuclear waste safer, instead of building a place to store it while it is still dangerous.

Other issues revolve around water. As Nevada's population grows, water must be divided between farms, cities, and fish and other wildlife. Although there is a lot of water in the Colorado River, seven states (Arizona, Colorado, Utah, Wyoming, New Mexico, California, and Nevada) and two countries (Mexico and the United States) share it. The groundwater and river water that the rest of the state uses is limited.

Many Nevadans feel it is dangerous to store radioactive waste at Yucca Mountain, a desert area located in Nye County.

Water is a scarce resource in some parts of the West.

The United States government, local people, and Native Americans have different views about water use. Native Americans argue that enough water must flow from Nevada's rivers into terminal lakes and swamps to keep fish and other wildlife alive. Farmers and ranchers want enough irrigation water to care for their crops and animals. Each new person who moves to Nevada's cities and towns needs water, too. However, many of Nevada's lakes are shrinking. In dry years, swamps and sinks dry up. Farmers, city leaders, environmentalists, and Native Americans argue over who gets Nevada's water.

In spite of these issues, Nevada's population continues to grow. Growth brings exciting changes, too. There are more kinds of jobs in Nevada than there used to be. Large cities can support things such as symphony orchestras and professional sports teams. Nevada's challenge is to grow without losing the things that make it special. It has always been home to tough, independent people who can get the job done.

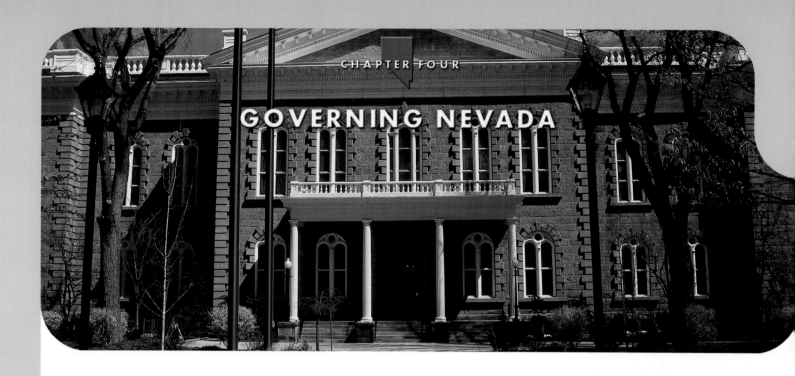

CHAPTER FOUR

GOVERNING NEVADA

Nevada's constitution was written during the Civil War. This important document defines the organization of Nevada's government, outlines the rights of the state's citizens, sets up counties, and makes rules for voting. It also creates rules for collecting taxes from residents of Nevada—money that is used for running the government and completing community projects. The Nevada constitution defines three branches of government: executive, legislative, and judicial.

The capitol building is a proud symbol of Nevada's state government.

EXECUTIVE BRANCH

The executive branch enforces state laws. The governor leads the executive branch. He or she sees that laws are carried out. The governor is elected for a four-year term and may serve for two terms, or eight years.

The governor works with other elected officials in the executive branch to carry out his or her duties. These officials include the lieutenant governor, the secretary of state, the attorney general, the controller, and the treasurer. They all serve four-year terms. The lieutenant governor runs the state if the governor is absent. The secretary of state keeps records of what the legislature does. The attorney general is the state's head law officer. He or she reviews state laws and helps to enforce them. The treasurer and the controller keep track of Nevada's money.

Nevada's lawmakers meet in the state legislative building in Carson City.

LEGISLATIVE BRANCH

The legislative branch, also called the legislature, makes laws. It also sets taxes and decides how to spend tax money. The Nevada legislature has two parts, called houses. The assembly has forty-two members, called representatives. The senate has twenty-one members, called senators. Assembly members serve two-year terms, and state senators serve four-year terms. All legislators must be at least twenty-one years old and have lived in Nevada for one year when they are elected. Legislators may not serve more than twelve years in office.

NEVADA GOVERNORS

Name	Term	Name	Term
James Warren Nye (territorial governor)	1861–1864	James Graves Scrugham	1923–1927
Henry Goode Blasdel	1864–1871	Frederick Bennett Balzar	1927–1934
Lewis Rice Bradley	1871–1879	Morley Isaac Griswold	1934–1935
John Henry Kinkead	1879–1883	Richard Kirman	1935–1939
Jewett William Adams	1883–1887	Edward Peter Carville	1939–1945
Charles Clark Stevenson	1887–1890	Vail Montgomery Pittman	1945–1951
Frank Bell	1890–1891	Charles Hinton Russell	1951–1959
Roswell Keyes Colcord	1891–1895	Frank "Grant" Sawyer	1959–1967
John Edward Jones	1895–1896	Paul Dominique Laxalt	1967–1971
Reinhold Sadler	1896–1903	Donald Neil "Mike" O'Callaghan	1971–1979
John Sparks	1903–1908	Robert Frank List	1979–1983
Denver Sylvester Dickerson	1908–1911	Richard Hudson Bryan	1983–1989
Tasker Lowndes Oddie	1911–1915	Robert Joseph Miller	1989–1999
Emmet Derby Boyle	1915–1923	Kenny C. Guinn	1999–

The Nevada legislature meets every other year. Lawmakers must finish their work in 120 days. The rest of the time legislators work on committees such as health care, radioactive waste, or public lands, in order to research these topics and make recommendations for new state laws.

When legislators or other government officials have an idea for a law, they begin by writing it down. The bill, or suggested law, is read to the assembly or the senate, depending on which house it was introduced in. It is then sent to a related committee. For example, bills about teachers go to the education committee.

The committee members read the law and suggest that it be passed, revised (changed), or not voted on. Bills that are recommended by the committee are discussed and voted on by legislators. If legislators vote in favor of a bill, it is sent to the governor for approval. The governor may either sign the bill into law or veto (reject) it.

If the governor vetoes a bill, it goes back to the legislature and is voted on again. If two in three legislators in both houses approve the bill, then it becomes a law. In Nevada, if the governor does not sign or veto a bill within five days, it becomes law.

WHO'S WHO IN NEVADA?

Harry Reid (1939–) grew up in Searchlight, in a house without running water. The town didn't have a high school, so he boarded with families in Henderson to finish school. He went to law school and eventually worked his way up in politics. He served in the Nevada State Assembly before being elected Nevada's youngest lieutenant governor in 1970. In 1986, Nevadans elected him a United States senator. During his successful terms in office he made many important contributions to Nevada.

JUDICIAL BRANCH

The judicial branch interprets, or explains, the law. This branch

NEVADA STATE GOVERNMENT

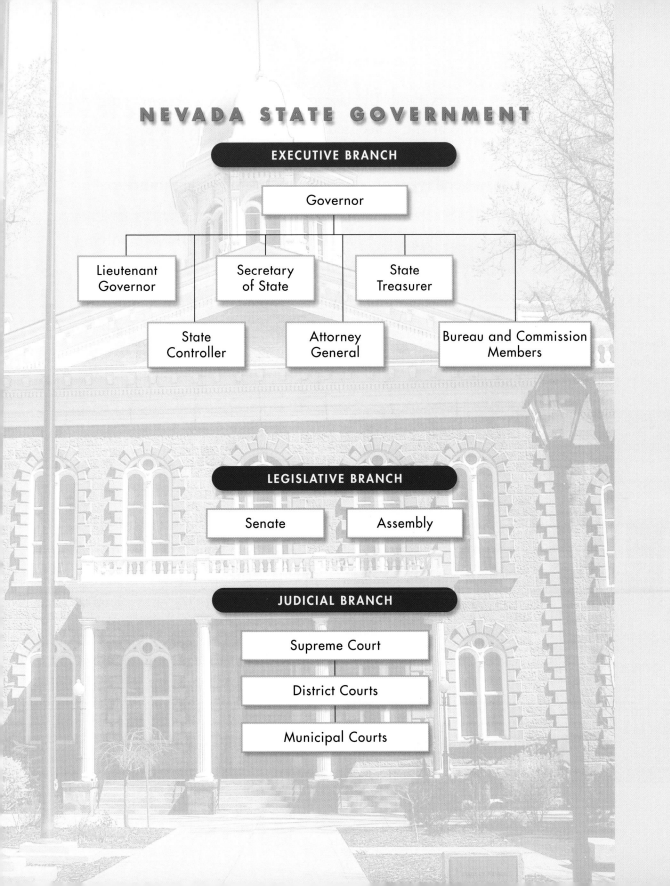

EXECUTIVE BRANCH

Governor

Lieutenant Governor

Secretary of State

State Treasurer

State Controller

Attorney General

Bureau and Commission Members

LEGISLATIVE BRANCH

Senate

Assembly

JUDICIAL BRANCH

Supreme Court

District Courts

Municipal Courts

resolves disagreements about the law and determines a person's guilt or innocence when he or she is accused of breaking a law. These responsibilities are carried out through the court system.

Nevada has several types of courts. Many cases begin in municipal or justice courts. These courts hear cases involving minor crimes, such as jaywalking and speeding. Criminal trials—for example, those involving robbery or murder—are heard in district courts. District courts also hear major civil cases. Civil cases usually involve disagreements between two or more people about land, money, contracts, or family matters. There are more than fifty district court judges in Nevada. They are elected for six-year terms.

The highest court of law in Nevada is the state supreme court.

If a person is not satisfied with the decision made in district court, he or she may appeal, or ask a higher court to review the case to see if any mistakes were made. Nevada has only one court of appeals, the Nevada Supreme Court. The supreme court is also responsible for overseeing lawyers who practice in the state and for making improvements in Nevada's judicial system. The supreme court has six judges and a chief justice who serve six-year terms.

Carson City had a population of 52,457 in 2000. It is 30 miles (48 km) south of Reno, near the silver mines that brought early settlers to Nevada. You can learn a lot about Nevada's history in Carson City. Many of the old buildings have been restored and are now used for government offices. Newer buildings house the legislature, the state supreme court, and the Nevada State Library.

The capitol is in the center of town. It was finished in 1871 and is built from Nevada sandstone. Inside, you'll see French crystal windows and Alaskan marble. The dome on Nevada's capitol building is silver-colored. Legend says it is real silver, but the capitol's caretakers say it is just silver paint.

Inside, the walls of the capitol are lined with portraits of Nevada's governors. The governor's office is downstairs. Upstairs there is a small museum that includes a huge chair made of elk horns. The chair belonged to Governor John Sparks. President Teddy Roosevelt sat in it when he visited Nevada in 1903.

Take a walk to the Nevada State Museum in the old Carson City Mint building, which closed in 1893. You can see samples of all the coins made at the mint or make your own coin in a special machine. The museum also includes a re-created mining town.

The silver dome of the capitol building is Carson City's most visible landmark.

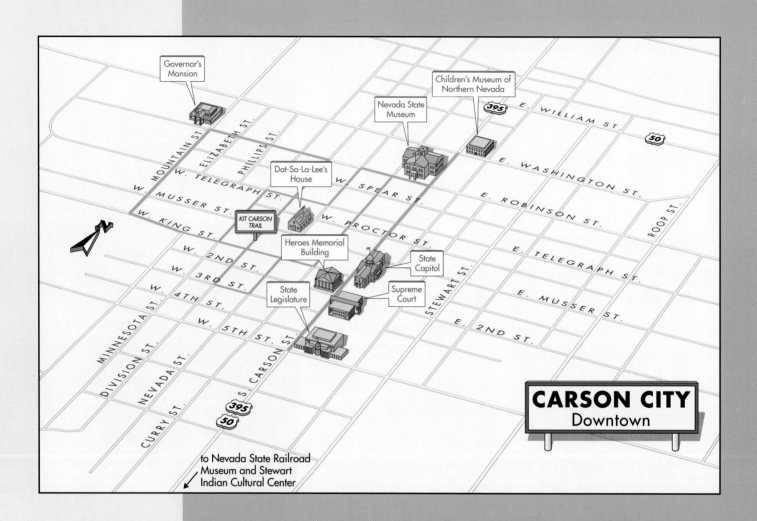

Governor's Mansion

Children's Museum of Northern Nevada

Nevada State Museum

Dat-So-La-Lee's House

KIT CARSON TRAIL

Heroes Memorial Building

State Capitol

State Legislature

Supreme Court

CARSON CITY
Downtown

to Nevada State Railroad Museum and Stewart Indian Cultural Center

MOUNTAIN ST.
ELIZABETH ST.
PHILLIPS ST.
W. TELEGRAPH ST.
W. MUSSER ST.
W. KING ST.
W. 2ND ST.
W. 3RD ST.
W. 4TH ST.
W. 5TH ST.
S. CARSON ST.
W. SPEAR ST.
W. PROCTOR ST.
STEWART ST.
MINNESOTA ST.
DIVISION ST.
NEVADA ST.
CURRY ST.

E. WILLIAM ST.
E. WASHINGTON ST.
E. ROBINSON ST.
E. TELEGRAPH ST.
E. MUSSER ST.
E. 2ND ST.
ROOP ST.

395
50

Outside the museum, follow a blue line on the sidewalk along the Kit Carson Trail. Carson City is named for explorer Kit Carson. He traveled through the valley where Carson City is located while he was exploring Nevada. The trail takes you past historic homes, churches, and buildings. If you prefer to drive the trail, you can still get lots of information about the city's history from the "talking houses." Twenty-four historic homes broadcast information about the houses, their owners, and their history right to your car radio from special transmitters. One talking house belonged to Dat-So-La-Lee, the famous Washo basket maker from Carson City.

You can learn about American Indian history at the Stewart Indian Museum in the old Stewart Indian School. The school operated from 1890 to 1980. You will learn how Native American children were taken from their homes, often against their parents' wishes, and educated at boarding schools like this one.

How would you like to have a birthday party in a caboose? It's possible at the Nevada State Railroad Museum. The museum, at the south end of Carson City, has

A statue of scout Kit Carson stands on the grounds of the capitol building.

WHO'S WHO IN NEVADA?

Dat-So-La-Lee (c. 1835–1925), born Dabuda, was a Washo woman who grew up near today's Carson City. As a girl, she learned to weave baskets, and eventually she became a skilled artist. Around 1905, Abe Cohn, who lived in Carson City, helped her sell the baskets. She signed them with the name Dat-So-La-Lee. Her beautiful baskets are now displayed in many museums.

The Inyo is the oldest operating steam engine in America.

sixty-five locomotives and cars. Most were part of the Virginia and Truckee Railroad, which ran to Carson City, Virginia City, and Reno. You'll see the Inyo, the oldest operating locomotive in the United States. Many of the locomotives in the museum have been in movies and on television. Today they carry visitors on rides.

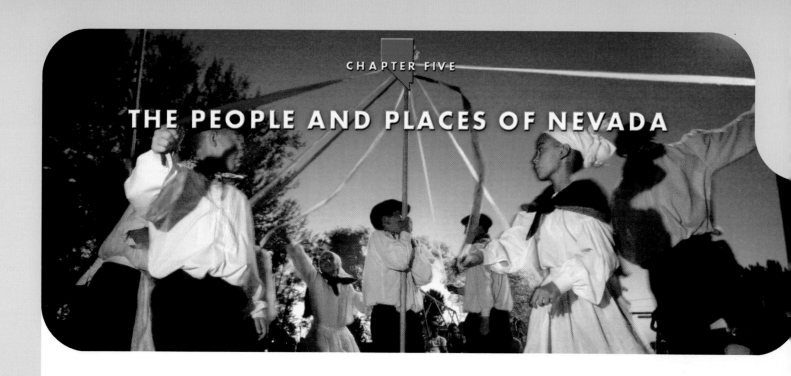

CHAPTER FIVE

THE PEOPLE AND PLACES OF NEVADA

Nevadans include a variety of people—buckaroos roping calves, Mexican folk dancers spinning their skirts, and Washo weaving baskets. New people join them every day. In 2000, Nevada was the nation's fastest-growing state.

In 2000, there were 1,998,257 people living in Nevada. Nevada has a low population density, which means that a small number of people live in each square mile of the state. In fact, only seven states have more space for each person than Nevada. There are blocks in Reno or Las Vegas where hundreds of people live in apartments, and there are miles and miles in rural Nevada where no one lives.

Most Nevadans live in urban areas, or cities. Almost 7 in 10 Nevadans live in the cities and suburbs of Las Vegas and Henderson. About 2 in 10 people live in Reno, Sparks, and Carson City in western

Basque dancers perform a maypole dance at Lion's Park in Battle Mountain.

Nevada. Only about 1 in 10 Nevadans live in the rest of the state. Small towns and out-of-the-way ranches are spread across rural Nevada.

Most Nevadans (7 in 10) are of European descent. Their ancestors came from Ireland, Germany, Italy, or other European countries. Almost 1 in 5 people are Latino or Hispanic. Their families came from Spanish-speaking countries such as Mexico or Chile. About 4 in 100 Nevadans have Asian backgrounds, and 7 in 100 are African-American.

Fewer than 2 in 100 Nevadans are Native American. Many Native Americans live on reservations in rural areas. Towns such as Nixon, Schurtz, and Dresslerville are on reservations.

Las Vegas provides many opportunities for tourism-related jobs. Below, tourists enjoy a gondola ride at Grand Canal Shoppes.

WORKING IN NEVADA

In 2002, almost half of all working Nevadans had service jobs. Many of the state's service jobs rely on tourism, which is the business of providing food, shelter, and entertainment for visitors. Almost 1 in 4 Nevadans work in the tourist industry. Tourists enjoy gambling in Nevada—there are slot machines in gas stations, restaurants, and even supermarkets! Las Vegas alone had more than 35 million visitors in 2000. The city has more than 125,000 hotel rooms and nine of the ten largest hotels in the world. Working Nevadans clean hotel rooms, cook for restaurants, and entertain visitors.

Other service workers provide health care, business services, and legal services to people who live in Nevada. About 1 in 20 Nevadans works in the transportation and communications industries. Many companies, such as Amazon.com and Porsche, have warehouses in Nevada. Truckers drive goods across the West. Many Nevadans also work in construction, building homes and businesses. In 2002, about 1 in 10 Nevadans worked in construction jobs. They may work as carpenters, plumbers, or electricians.

About 1 in 20 Nevadans works in manufacturing. These Nevadans make things that are shipped across the country and around the world. Things that are made in Nevada include cat litter, computer parts, gambling equipment, and candy. J. M. Capriola Company in Elko claims to be one of the only places in the world that makes and repairs saddles and gear for working cowboys.

In 2002, about 9,000 Nevadans worked in mining. They uncover materials such as gold, silver, copper, barite, cement, gypsum, and limestone. Although Nevada still produces more minerals than most other states, many mines have closed. When prices drop on some metals and ores, or if mining gets more difficult and more expensive to do, the mines make changes to save money. In 2002, about 1 in 10 Nevada miners lost a job.

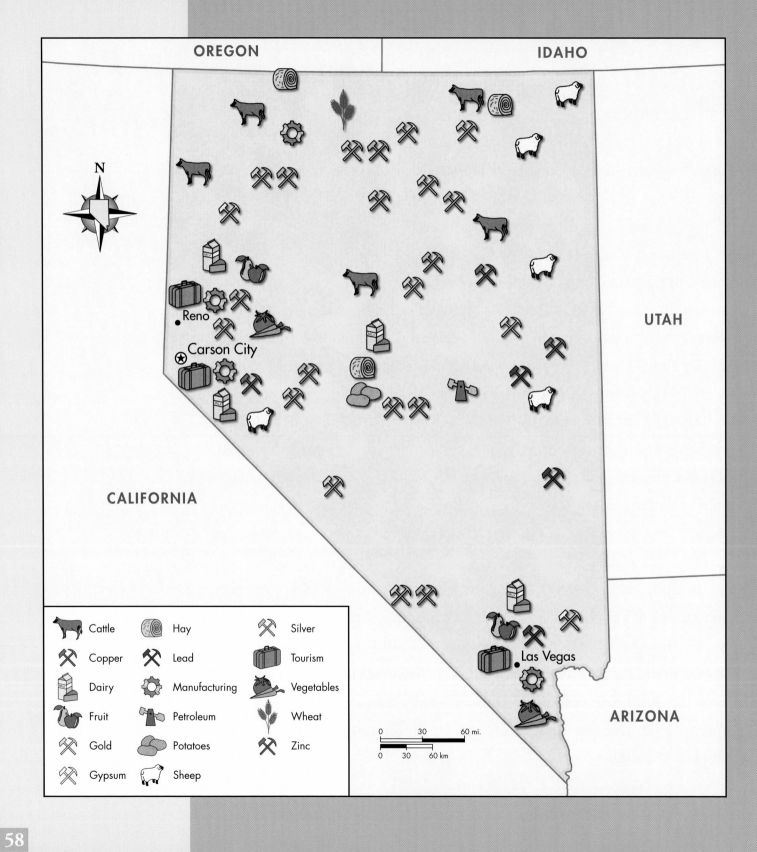

OREGON

IDAHO

N

Reno

Carson City

CALIFORNIA

UTAH

Las Vegas

ARIZONA

	Cattle		Hay		Silver
	Copper		Lead		Tourism
	Dairy		Manufacturing		Vegetables
	Fruit		Petroleum		Wheat
	Gold		Potatoes		Zinc
	Gypsum		Sheep		

0   30   60 mi.

0   30   60 km

A cowboy herds cattle near Battle Mountain, a small community with a long tradition of ranching.

Some Nevadans are farmers or ranchers. About 2 in 1,000 people own farms; others work on the farms, raising cattle and sheep. Crops include alfalfa, nursery plants, melons, and vegetables. Farmers often live in small towns or on ranches miles away from their neighbors.

TAKE A TOUR OF NEVADA

Nevada has two urban areas: Las Vegas and Reno/Sparks/Carson City. Outside these areas, many of Nevada's roads go for miles without passing by a town, or even a gas station. But don't pass them up—some of Nevada's best spots are miles down dirt or gravel roads! To see Nevada, you have to explore. Let's begin our tour in Las Vegas.

EXTRA! EXTRA!

The town of McDermitt may be small, but some of its residents have a big job. High-school students from this ranching community provide Internet access for people living in the surrounding area. The McDermitt Combined School students' Internet company provides service to Humboldt County, Nevada, and Malheur County, Oregon. These students are not only learning valuable skills, they are also providing an important service to their community.

Las Vegas is Nevada's biggest city, and possibly the world's brightest. Casinos line the Las Vegas Strip. The 3-mile- (4.8-km-) long Strip has 15,000 miles (24,140 km) of neon tubing in its lights. More than 35 million people visit Las Vegas every year. Adults gamble in the casinos and enjoy world-famous entertainment. Meanwhile, young people can ride a roller coaster outside the New York New York casino or see a clown or high-wire act at Circus Circus. You can also visit the Ethel M. Chocolate Factory. Inside the factory, visitors can watch chocolate pouring over the candy fillings at the chocolate "car wash." A dryer blows the chocolate dry.

The neon signs of the Strip advertise hotels, restaurants, and entertainment.

You can also visit the Southern Nevada Zoo. The small park has 150 species of plants and animals. At Ron Lee's World of Clowns in Henderson, take a tour to see how animated clowns and sculptures are made. Stop in on Friday or Saturday night to see the planetarium show at the Community College of Southern Nevada Planetarium in North Las Vegas. You may learn about the stars, the planets, or the search for intelligent life in other worlds.

Over thousands of years, wind and water erosion have created dramatic formations such as Elephant Rock at Valley of Fire State Park.

Not far from Las Vegas, tour buses, trucks, and cars wind down a steep canyon toward Hoover Dam. You can put on a hard hat and take a tour inside the dam. Behind the dam, you can go boating on Lake Mead.

Valley of Fire State Park is nearby, where huge red rocks twist and arch beside the road. They have names such as Beehive and Elephant Rock. You can also see where an outlaw lived at Mouse's Tank or hike along a tiny creek that bubbles over the rocks. Cacti and wildflowers bloom at your feet.

Rhyolite, north of Las Vegas, was once the center of a booming mining district. Today it is a ghost town. All that is left are the stone skeletons of its buildings. There are sculptures of ghosts riding bicycles and driving cars around the town.

Rhyolite is famous for its Bottle House. A miner built this house using empty bottles from the town saloons, held together with mud and plaster. All the bottles kept the little house cool. However, the builder never lived in the house—instead, he held a raffle and gave the house to the winner!

Two favorite spots for families are Red Rock Canyon on the west side of town, and Mount Charleston north of the city. In Red Rock Canyon, hikers enjoy blue skies. Mount Charleston rises high above the desert. Pine trees grow on the mountain. On hot days, it is a cool place for a picnic.

Drive north from Las Vegas to discover a hidden corner of southeast Nevada. Outside Caliente, visit Rainbow Canyon. You'll be surprised at the colorful rocks and the peaceful creek. Cathedral Gorge State Park has chalky cliffs that rise like church walls from flat meadow-land. Then drive down a dirt road to Beaver Dam State Park. It seems like a water world in the desert. Birds settle on ponds, and rabbits speed across paths. You're a long way from Las Vegas!

Each year, millions of visitors take in the sights of Reno.

Reno and Western Nevada

Reno is called the Biggest Little City in the World. For a city of 180,480 people, there's a lot to do.

Downtown, you can visit the National Auto Museum. There are more than 220 old and antique cars in the museum. The cars are displayed in street scenes that show what life was like when they were fashionable. A few blocks away, the National Bowling Stadium holds hundreds of bowling events.

If you get tired of crowds, you can ski, hike, river-raft, bike, and rock hound near Reno. Lake Tahoe and Pyramid Lake are close by. Thousands of visitors play at Lake Tahoe. They swim and boat in summer. In winter, skiers and snowboarders can choose from many ski resorts. Pyramid Lake, north of Reno, is known for fishing.

Summertime is fun time in Reno. In June, the rodeo comes to town, and cowboys from around the country compete in events such as bronc riding, calf roping, and bull riding. In July, the Art Town Festival celebrates art, music, theater, and dance.

A bronc rider holds on tight during a competition in the Reno Rodeo.

Every August, thousands of classic-car lovers from around the United States gather for Hot August Nights. Crowds turn out to see 5,000 cars cruising the streets, including Model Ts, 1956 Chevys, and old milk trucks. Some people dress up in poodle skirts or letter jackets and ride in 1950s cars.

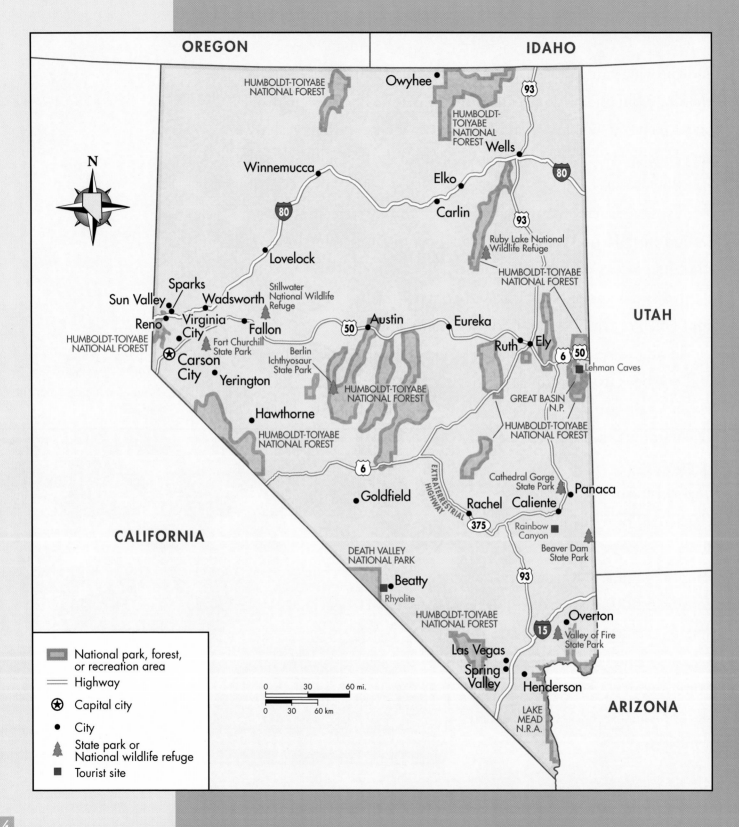

OREGON

IDAHO

HUMBOLDT-TOIYABE
NATIONAL FOREST

Owyhee

93

HUMBOLDT-
TOIYABE
NATIONAL
FOREST

Wells

N

Winnemucca

Elko

80

Carlin

93

UTAH

Ruby Lake National
Wildlife Refuge

HUMBOLDT-TOIYABE
NATIONAL FOREST

Lovelock

Sparks

Sun Valley

Wadsworth

Stillwater
National Wildlife
Refuge

HUMBOLDT-TOIYABE
NATIONAL FOREST

Reno

Virginia
City

Fallon

50

Austin

Eureka

Ruth

Ely

6

50

Fort Churchill
State Park

Carson
City

Yerington

Berlin
Ichthyosaur
State Park

HUMBOLDT-TOIYABE
NATIONAL FOREST

Lehman Caves

GREAT BASIN
N.P.

HUMBOLDT-TOIYABE
NATIONAL FOREST

Hawthorne

HUMBOLDT-TOIYABE
NATIONAL FOREST

6

Cathedral Gorge
State Park

Panaca

Goldfield

EXTRATERRESTRIAL HIGHWAY

Rachel

Caliente

CALIFORNIA

375

Rainbow
Canyon

Beaver Dam
State Park

DEATH VALLEY
NATIONAL PARK

93

Beatty

Rhyolite

HUMBOLDT-TOIYABE
NATIONAL FOREST

Overton

15

Valley of Fire
State Park

Las Vegas

Spring
Valley

Henderson

ARIZONA

LAKE
MEAD
N.R.A.

National park, forest,
or recreation area

Highway

Capital city

City

State park or
National wildlife refuge

Tourist site

0   30   60 mi.

0   30   60 km

In September, folks who get up early can watch more than one hundred balloons take off from Reno's Rancho San Rafael Park in the Great Reno Balloon Race. Families bring breakfast and wander among the balloons as the pilots and crews fill them with hot air. The balloons lift off after sunrise.

On the same day, Virginia City holds the International Camel Races. Camels once carried salt and mail in Nevada. Today they lurch around a dusty track as riders hang on for dear life. After the races, you can tour historic Piper's Opera House or the Mackay Mansion, which mining millionaire John Mackay built for his family. You can also take a short locomotive ride on the Virginia and Truckee Railroad, or have an ice cream soda along the Virginia City boardwalk.

The Genoa Candy Dance is a fall tradition. It has been held every year since the early 1900s, when women from Genoa (Mormon Station) made and sold candy, then held a dance. They used the money they made to buy streetlights for their town. These days, thousands of people visit Genoa in late September to buy candy and crafts.

Hot-air balloons take flight above Reno.

North and Central Nevada

Elko, in north-central Nevada, is the center of a ranching and mining community. You may see a real cowboy carrying his saddle down the

Lehman Caves is a beautiful limestone cavern with unusual formations.

street. You can hear cowboys reading poetry at the National Cowboy Poetry Gathering in January. More than eight thousand people from around the world attend. Then, warm up with dinner at a Basque restaurant. You'll sit family-style at long tables and pass around bowls piled with food. Most Basque restaurants serve all you can eat.

In Ely you can ride the Ghost Train, an old steam locomotive. Plan to visit Great Basin National Park. You can hike to the bristlecone pines on Wheeler Peak. The steep trail takes you above the forest to the rocky slopes where the ancient bristlecone pine trees live. You can also tour Lehman Caves. Watch for bats!

You should always carry water on Nevada's back roads and trails. A snack won't hurt either! This trail mix uses a familiar Nevada ingredient—pine nuts. It also uses M&M's®, which you can mix yourself at M&M® World on the Strip in Las Vegas. Enjoy!

NEVADA TRAIL MIX

2 cups granola
1/2 cup pine nuts (or peanuts)
1/2 cup M&Ms®
1/2 cup raisins

1. Stir all ingredients together in a bowl.
2. Scoop single servings into plastic bags. Eat on the trail!

Midway across Highway 50 in Nevada is the small town of Austin. It was once a busy mining town. South of Austin, miles down a dirt road, is Berlin Ichthyosaur State Park. Berlin is an old ghost town where you can peer at spider webs, tin cans, and tools in deserted miners' cabins. On the mountain above Berlin, you'll see fossils of ichthyosaurs that once swam in Lake Lahontan.

You can see birds nesting at the Stillwater National Wildlife Refuge near Fallon. Look for flocks of big American white pelicans circling overhead or landing on the marsh. During some years, the marsh is dry.

At Fallon, head south to visit Fort Churchill State Park near Yerrington. The fort was built of adobe—mud and grass bricks that are baked until hard—with wooden roofs. When the army closed Fort Churchill, people took the wood from the roofs. Without roofs, the fort's adobe buildings have melted toward the ground. They stand like strange sculptures framed by trees along the Carson River.

Fort Churchill was once a U.S. Army fort built to provide protection for the area's early settlers.

State Highway 375, the Extraterrestrial Highway, runs from near Alamo in the east to near Tonopah in the west. It is so empty, some people claim it is visited by unidentified flying objects (UFOs). Road signs along Highway 375 include a picture of a little alien. Other signs tell of upcoming trash cans—there is nothing else to mark for miles. The tiny town of Rachael, midway on the Extraterrestrial Highway, is supposed to be a good place to spot UFOs.

Drive west from Tonopah along Highway 6 toward the California border. As you leave Nevada, you'll see a sign painted on a water tank: "We miss you already." Come back soon!

NEVADA ALMANAC

Statehood date and number: October 31, 1864; the 36th state

State seal: Features a scene of early mines, railroads, and farms on a mountain background. At the bottom are the words "All for Our Country." Adopted in 1866.

State flag: Has a blue background, with sagebrush crossed to form a half wreath in the upper left corner. Across the top of the wreath is a golden scroll with the words "Battle Born, Nevada." A silver star is in the middle of the wreath. Adopted in 1929.

Geographic center: Lander County, 26 miles (42 km) southeast of Austin

Total area/rank: 110,567 square miles (286,367 sq km)/7th

Borders: Oregon, Idaho, Utah, Arizona, California

Latitude and longitude: Nevada is located between 35° and 42° N and 114° 02' and 120° W

Highest/lowest elevation: Boundary Peak, 13,140 feet (4,005 m) above sea level/the Colorado River in Clark County, 479 feet (146 m) above sea level

Hottest/coldest temperature: 125° F (52° C) at Laughlin on June 29, 1994/–50° F (–45.5° C) at San Jacinto on January 8, 1937

Land area/rank: 109,826 square miles (284,448 sq km)/7th

Inland water area/rank: 761 square miles (1,971 sq km)/34th

Population/rank (2000 census): 1,998,257/35th

Population of major cities:
- **Las Vegas:** 478,434
- **Reno:** 180,480
- **Henderson:** 175,381
- **North Las Vegas:** 115,488

Origin of state name: Spanish for "snowy"

State capital: Carson City

Counties: 16, and 1 independent city (Carson City)

State government: 21 senators, 42 representatives

Major rivers/lakes: Truckee, Humboldt, Carson, Colorado, Walker, Reese, Bruneau, Owyhee, Salmon/Tahoe, Pyramid, Walker, Mead

Farm products: Alfalfa, potatoes, onions, garlic, barley, wheat

Livestock: Cattle, sheep

Manufactured products: Food products, plastics, chemicals, aerospace products, irrigation equipment

Mining products: Silver, gold, copper, sand and gravel, diatomite

Animal: Desert bighorn sheep

Artifact: Tule duck

Bird: Mountain bluebird

Colors: Silver and blue

Fish: Lahontan cutthroat trout

Flower: Sagebrush

Fossil: Ichthyosaur

Grass: Indian rice grass

Metal: Silver

Motto: "All for Our Country"

Nicknames: Silver State, Sagebrush State, Battle Born State

Precious gemstone: Virgin Valley black fire opal

Reptile: Desert tortoise

Rock: Sandstone

Semiprecious gemstone: Nevada turquoise

Song: "Home Means Nevada," by Bertha Raffetto

Trees: Single-leaf piñon, bristlecone pine

Wildlife: Coyotes, rabbits, antelope, deer, bighorn sheep, bears, birds, snakes

TIMELINE

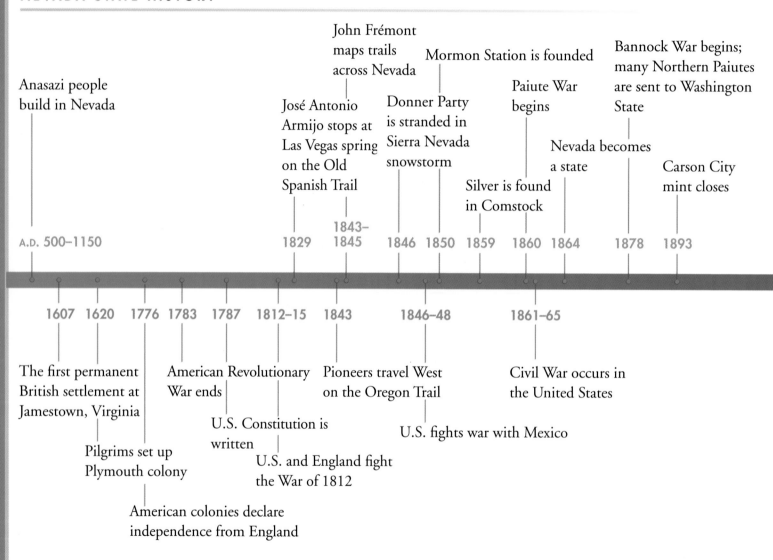

A.D. 500–1150 — Anasazi people build in Nevada

1829 — José Antonio Armijo stops at Las Vegas spring on the Old Spanish Trail

1843–1845 — John Frémont maps trails across Nevada

1846 — Donner Party is stranded in Sierra Nevada snowstorm

1850 — Mormon Station is founded

1859 — Silver is found in Comstock

1860 — Paiute War begins

1864 — Nevada becomes a state

1878 — Bannock War begins; many Northern Paiutes are sent to Washington State

1893 — Carson City mint closes

1607 — The first permanent British settlement at Jamestown, Virginia

1620 — Pilgrims set up Plymouth colony

1776 — American colonies declare independence from England

1783 — American Revolutionary War ends

1787 — U.S. Constitution is written

1812–15 — U.S. and England fight the War of 1812

1843 — Pioneers travel West on the Oregon Trail

1846–48 — U.S. fights war with Mexico

1861–65 — Civil War occurs in the United States

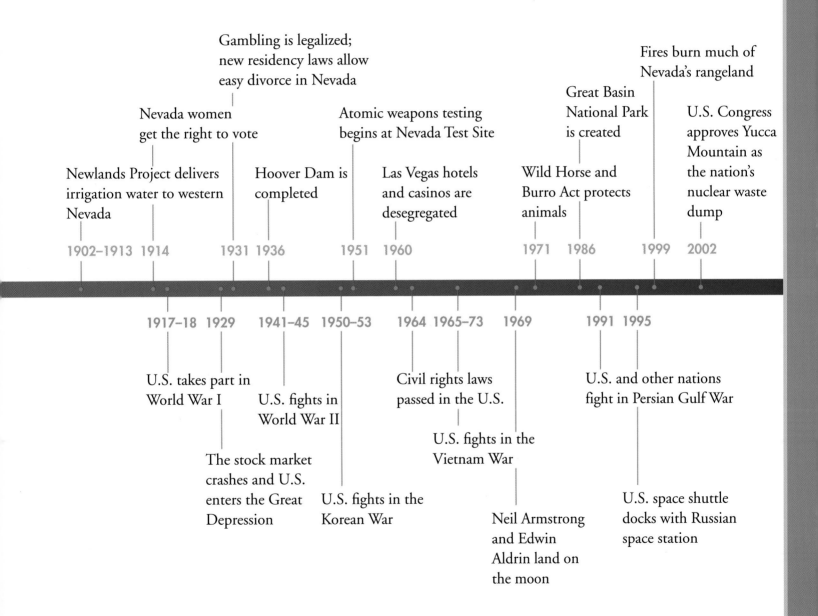

Gambling is legalized;
new residency laws allow
easy divorce in Nevada

Nevada women
get the right to vote

Atomic weapons testing
begins at Nevada Test Site

Great Basin
National Park
is created

Fires burn much of
Nevada's rangeland

U.S. Congress
approves Yucca
Mountain as
the nation's
nuclear waste
dump

Newlands Project delivers
irrigation water to western
Nevada

Hoover Dam is
completed

Las Vegas hotels
and casinos are
desegregated

Wild Horse and
Burro Act protects
animals

1902–1913 1914   1931 1936   1951 1960   1971 1986   1999 2002

1917–18 1929   1941–45 1950–53   1964 1965–73   1969   1991 1995

U.S. takes part in
World War I

U.S. fights in
World War II

Civil rights laws
passed in the U.S.

U.S. and other nations
fight in Persian Gulf War

The stock market
crashes and U.S.
enters the Great
Depression

U.S. fights in the
Vietnam War

U.S. fights in the
Korean War

Neil Armstrong
and Edwin
Aldrin land on
the moon

U.S. space shuttle
docks with Russian
space station

73

GALLERY OF FAMOUS NEVADANS

Andre Agassi

(1970–)

International tennis star and Las Vegas community supporter. Agassi has raised more than $10 million to help the city's young people. Born in Las Vegas.

Robert Laxalt

(1924–2001)

A respected writer, known for writing about Basque culture and Nevada. Lived in Reno.

Moya Lear

(1915–2001)

Widow of inventor Bill Lear, Moya Lear was a well-known supporter of the arts and education. Lived in Reno.

John Mackay

(1831–1902)

Mine owner and community leader. Mackay's family donated much money to help build the University of Nevada in Reno. Lived in Virginia City.

Anne Martin

(1875–1951)

Leader in the Nevada Equal Franchise Society, which worked for women's voting rights. Also the first woman to run for the United States Senate, in 1918 and 1920. Born in Empire.

Wayne Newton

(1942–)

Famous entertainer in Las Vegas, where he has performed more than 25,000 shows. He is called Mr. Las Vegas.

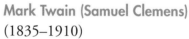

Emma Sepulveda

(1950–)

Writer, Hispanic community leader, and professor at the University of Nevada, Reno. Lives in Reno.

Mark Twain (Samuel Clemens)

(1835–1910)

One of America's most famous writers. His books include *The Adventures of Tom Sawyer, The Adventures of Huckleberry Finn,* and *Roughing It,* a book about the two years he spent in Nevada. Lived in Carson City and Virginia City.

Steve Wynn

(1942–)

Moved to Las Vegas when he was ten years old and grew up to be a resort builder and owner. His vision helped turn Las Vegas into a super resort city.

GLOSSARY

adobe: mud and straw building material

amendment: a revision or change made in a law, a constitution, etc.

ancestor: relative who lived long ago

canal: a man-made ditch used for carrying water

constitution: the plan, or rules, for a government

drought: a long period without rain or other precipitation

emigrant: person who traveled from one country or region to live in another

evaporation: the process in which a solid or a liquid substance turns into vapor, or dries up

geothermal: heated by the earth

geyser: a spring that throws up jets of hot water and steam periodically

integration: people of all races working and living together

irrigate: to bring water to dry land

ore: rocks that include precious or desired metals

petroglyphs: rock drawings made by ancient Native Americans

prospector: a person who searches for gold, silver, etc.

pueblo: a type of many-roomed house or apartment built by some Native Americans

radiation: energy in the form of heat and light

reservoir: a place to store a lot of water, often a man-made lake

rural: relating to the countryside, or people living there

sink: place where river water evaporates and sinks into the desert

suburb: neighborhoods and towns around a larger city

transcontinental: across the continent

wash: a dry riverbed that runs when it rains

FOR MORE INFORMATION

Web sites

Churchill County Museum and Archives, Indian Ways and Traditons Recalled
www.ccmuseum.org/InFocus/Hooper/hooper1.htm
A tribal member's account of Northern Paiute traditions and language.

Hoover Dam
www.usbr.gov/lc/hooverdam
Information about Hoover Dam, including facts for kids.

Las Vegas Review Journal, The First 100
www.1st100.com
Biographies of important southern Nevadans.

Department of Cultural Affairs, Nevada Kids Page
dmla.clan.lib.nv.us/docs/kids
Provides links to Nevada facts and photos.

Nevada State Home Page
www.nv.gov
General information about Nevada, and links to state government agencies.

Books

Dutemple, Lesley A. *The Hoover Dam.* Minneapolis: Lerner, 2003.

Lasky, Kathryn. *A Brilliant Streak: The Making of Mark Twain.* New York: Harcourt Brace, 1998.

Scordato, Ellen. *Sarah Winnemucca: Northern Paiute Writer and Diplomat.* New York: Chelsea House, 1992.

Wachtel, Roger. *The Donner Party.* Danbury: Children's Press, 2003.

Addresses

Nevada Commission on Tourism
401 North Carson Street
Carson City, NV 89701

Nevada Governor's Office
State Capitol Building
Carson City, NV 89701

Nevada State Museum
600 North Carson Street
Carson City, NV 89701

INDEX

ABOUT THE AUTHOR

Suzanne M. Williams can see the sun rise over Mount Davidson from her window. To research this book, she ate in Basque restaurants, visited Rachael on the Extraterrestrial Highway, and hiked through Beaver Dam State Park. She also talked to fellow Nevadans, read books, and surfed the Web. She finds all parts of Nevada exciting, including gnarled bristlecone pines, dams that changed the Southwest, and a buckaroo carrying his saddle down a silent road.

Photographs © 2003: AP/Wide World Photos: 53 (Cathleen Allison/Nevada Appeal), 55 (Joe Cavaretta), 63 (Brian Corley/Nevada Appeal), 54 (Bill Husa/Nevada Appeal), 44 (Steve Marcus), 43 (Laura Rauch), 39 bottom; Brown Brothers: 27, 41 top; Carolyn Fox: 65, 71 top left; Corbis Images: 70 right (Morton Beebe), 23, 37, 38 (Bettmann), 46 (Mark E. Gibson), 35 (W.J. Lubken), 74 top right (Neal Preston), 56 (Reuters NewMedia Inc.), 41 bottom (Galen Rowell), 3 left, 8 top, 14, 68 (Scott T. Smith), 51 (Joseph Sohm/Visions of America), 39 top (UPI); Courtesy Secretary of State: 70 top left; David R. Frazier: 59; Dembinsky Photo Assoc./Scott T. Smith: 11; Denver Public Library, Western History Collection: 21 (Jedediah Smith on Horseback, by Frederic Remington, from the H.S. Poley Collection); Hulton|Archive/Getty Images: 34; Lynn M. Stone: 9 top; MapQuest.com, Inc.: 70 bottom left; Network Aspen: 74 top left (John Russell), 62; Nevada Historical Society: 26, 28 bottom, 28 top, 30, 33, 74 bottom left, 74 bottom right; Nevada State Museum: 19 (art by Karen Beyers, *Under One Sky Exhibition*); North Wind Picture Archives: 22, 25, 31; Photo Researchers, NY/Ron Sanford: 66; Stock Montage, Inc.: 17 top; Stone/Getty Images: 16 (Kim Blaxland), cover (Derek Gardner), 3 right, 4 (John Lamb), 9 bottom (David Muench), 60 (Donovan Reese); Superstock, Inc./Steve Vidler: 15; Tom Till Photography, Inc.: 13, 17 bottom, 61; Unicorn Stock Photos: 71 right (Dede Gilman), 45, 49 background (Paula J. Harrington); Viesti Collection, Inc.: 7 (Richard Cummins), 8 bottom, 12, 18, 50 (Robert Mitchell); Visuals Unlimited/Malowski: 71 bottom left.